MINE, OURS, and YOURS

A Father's Journey through
the Life and Death of a Child

Watson Jordan

Mine, Ours, and Yours: A Father's Journey through the Life and Death of a Child

Copyright © 2019 by Henry Watson Jordan
All rights reserved.
ISBN 9781072548072

Dedication

This book is dedicated to all the men who needed and wanted to grieve and heal, who looked for help and found none they could recognize—got mad, grew confused, gave up looking, and suffered … and suffered … and suffered
Know that you are not alone.

~ Watson

Special thanks to
Greg Vineyard for his insightful and revealing illustrations.
My editors Margo Warren and Ruth Olsen for encouragement.

FORWARD

by Mark M. Gordon

P ain, loss, injury, hurt, confusion, bewilderment, anxiety, sadness. These are states of being that we all fear and will do almost anything to avoid. The fact of being human is that these states of being will befall us all. The question is, how do we come to grips with unavoidable states of being human, and how do we respond.

In *Mine, Ours, and Yours*, Watson Jordan takes the uncommon step of a man sharing with the world his intimate injury, grapple, growth, and gift bestowed upon him through the death of his infant. Through his lens, Watson takes you on a walk through life. Life will happen to you without asking for advice or permission. Life greets you and you have only one choice: to forge on to the light. The light will shine upon you, but it must be sought.

Finding life's light can be complex. It's about you, but not all about you.

In *Mine, Ours, and Yours*, Watson shows us it's okay for a man to grieve. Our society has yet to fully affirm external male grief. Without using a hammer, Watson uses delicate narrative to let us into his mind and to read his thoughts about compassion, meaning, destiny, and obligation.

This short read is a vital read for multiple audiences: men who must grieve, caregivers who need to know the impact of one error, women who want to understand the emotions of injured males.

TABLE OF CONTENTS

INTRODUCTION

131.48 million feet. The distance around the earth is 131.48 million feet, which is 43.8 million yards. To put it another way, that's 2.92 million 15-yard lengths. Why 15 yards? That's the distance that my son Paul and I would throw the football back and forth to each other in our driveway. I have claimed that we threw that ball the distance around the earth. So, by my calculations, we threw 3 million passes. While doing this we also worked out each challenge and problem we faced. Many men like to talk this way … as part of an activity. Perhaps some of us are restless, which drives this behavior. Perhaps it harkens back to the days of a bear hunt.

The comedy show "Defending the Caveman" examined long-held perceptions of differences between men and women. Cavemen went off on a bear hunt. A hunt is active, tightly focused, with limited chatter. Cavewomen stayed in camp, cared for families and gathered: less active, broad focus, unlimited conversation. The show's idea was that today's generalities about the sexes tie to those long-ago centuries when our "hard wiring" was laid down.

There is something fundamentally ideal about men helping men grieve.

This short book is not a *how to* manual. Rather a story about how an injured man healed and folded his experience into the next moments and chapters of his life as a man, husband, and father. I wrote this for other men to read, to know what other fathers have faced and experienced. *To know that they are not alone.*

If I could, I would find a driveway with each one of them, find a football, throw it back and forth, and talk about it.

MINE

I backed my '85 Chevrolet Custom 10 Deluxe out of our driveway. The rebuilt transmission shifted into gear, and I headed back to work. As I crested over the first hill, the still small voice whispered, "Turn around, go home, and see if Meghan wants you to go with her." I stopped the truck, turned around, and headed home. The landscape and trajectory of our life and marriage was about to change in dramatic and unthinkable ways.

Eight months earlier, a colleague at the school where I worked learned that his third child was on the way. As we discussed our families in his office, he asked me how things were going. I easily and happily told him how happy Meghan and I were with our two children, how bright our future was, and how we were finished with pregnancy and babies. I was happy for him … but smugly pleased with our family size and makeup. How great things were.

Little did I know that we either were already pregnant or were soon to be—that the touch and feel of our daily life was about to shift dramatically. When the tests confirmed our third child was on the way, we looked at each other in disbelief. While we did not imagine an immaculate conception (that's what it seemed like) ... it did not seem possible that a third child was on the way. And yet …

The pregnancy triggered a cascade of events, the first was our having to move. We lived on the campus of the school where I worked, and our dorm apartment was exploding with life. We found a home close to school that needed a family. The purchase happened quickly and the renovation was fun and economical. We added a master bedroom, which brought the numbers of bedrooms to four. A bedroom each for our two children, Paul and Caroline, and the third room for the nursery, which in the end turned out to be one room too many. I worked that spring and summer preparing our new home. In July we moved our belongings and began to settle in. Meghan was comfortable; the children were thrilled, our dog Bickie was happy. I was content with our transition, pleased for the stable and quiet life of an off-campus house.

The school year began with great activity. School launchings are like a giant ocean liner leaving harbor. Lots of planning, days of meetings, too much hand-wringing … then finally the day arrives. It's a relief to actually begin the first day of school, rather than continue the incessant preparing for the students arrival! And it wasn't just the kids' prep, as I ran the technology department at school. No matter how much we planned, my department starts running behind in mid-August, gets further behind as September begins, and comes up for air when

October appears on the horizon. This September would be different.

August was like all of our Augusts, we returned from Vinalhaven, Maine, tanned and rested. The island quarry had cooled and refreshed us. Go Fish (the candy store) had provided treats and sugar highs. Upon our return, we launched into school preparation. Paul was in kindergarten and Caroline at Montessori pre-school. Meghan was nesting, and I had returned to work. A new school year in front of us ... football games ... pig pickings ... dress code ... convocations ... and chapels. My days began and concluded in darkness. Off to work early and home from work late ... a comfortable, familiar routine!

SO IT BEGINS

On occasion, I would return home for lunch. Our home was just a few minutes from school, and it was nice to see Meghan during the day when the kids were at school. But this day, it wasn't even lunchtime. That nudging voice had compelled me to turn the truck around before I even got to school. When I walked in the door, she was particularly glad to see me, and I could tell she wanted me to go with her to the appointment. Meghan spoke about the upcoming appointment. The moment I entered the house I could tell she wanted me to go with her. Perhaps she knew something was amiss

… maybe she was just lonely. In either event, she was glad to see me and relieved that I was going with her. I called school and let the department know I would be out for the afternoon.

This was our third child, so we were accustomed to the doctor's visits …
plenty of waiting
and wondering. It
was a sunny day.
We had a few
months to go
before the due date.
The nurse came
into the dark,
poorly-paneled
room. Following

the customary questions, she got out the ultrasound machine, smeared the jelly on Meghan's abdomen, and took a look.

As the nurse was looking at the ultrasound, she suddenly stopped, sat bolt upright, and excused herself. In just a few moments she returned with the doctor. Sometimes that kind of quick response is unwanted—no matter how much one dislikes waiting. Quickly, the doctor made a similar examination: she looked and silently confirmed what the nurse had reported. With a look of concern and shock, the doctor told us to pack up and go to the hospital. We were having the baby today.

Between the time we left the doctor's office and arrived at the hospital, much had happened. The instant we arrived we were rushed to a room. The boring comfort that comes from being healthy enough to wait our turn had vanished. In its place was tension and anxiety. We didn't know exactly what was going on—we didn't even know yet why the baby had to come so fast—we only knew that we were on the clock! Once we were in our room, the doctor arrived and did the ultrasound again. As she looked inside Meghan at our baby, she clenched her teeth and tried to hide her concern with that kind of canned bedside manner. Finally, she informed us that all the amniotic fluid was gone, and while not imminent, if the baby weren't delivered, it would die. An emergency C-section was planned. The operation would happen that afternoon.

As we waited, we thought more about the name and who would take care of our kids that night (they were two and five). We were months ahead of when we thought we needed answers to questions like this. We didn't even know our baby's gender. Margaret and William were names we'd discussed. William was a family name we liked, and Margaret was the name of my sister, who had died following childbirth. At this point, things were happening so quickly we were not actually scared—we were just trying to get our bearings. One thing was certain, I was in a completely different state of mind than a few months prior and the smug contentment I mentioned before. That afternoon's conversation with my friend was a world away now. Our third child was going to arrive, close to two months early. We were not ready—not even close.

Our friends Mark and Teresa carried us that day. They have two children, Bethany (Paul's age) and Zeb (Caroline's age). Teresa gathered the kids from Montessori and took care of the dog, Bickie. Mark worked at the hospital. He met us there and made certain we were okay and getting above-board care. I don't remember much about what we discussed, but I do remember Mark made sure I got something to eat. In retrospect, he may have known that we had a challenge in front of us.

BIRTH

We were told that we were having an emergency C-section—in 30 minutes! The upside to a short runway is that the time to worry is brief. Compared to the delivery of our first two children, the C-section was anti-climactic. Meghan was prepped, wheeled into the operating room, and cut open. They pulled our baby out. It was a boy and he was fine. My tiny son was okay; and I was exhausted and relieved.

We agreed earlier that I would follow the baby wherever he went. This meant leaving Meghan. We both agreed this was best, but it felt horrible.

He was quickly put into a carrier and wheeled directly to the neonatal intensive care unit (NICU). As we wheeled through the halls, I overheard the nurses talking about specific things they saw in William, more than his small size. When we arrived at the NICU, they checked William in and reviewed his arrival with the NICU staff. Then they pointed out that his tongue was sticking slightly out of his mouth. This is often associated with children who have Down syndrome. They said they would test him for that condition. We would have to wait for the results … until after the weekend.

Waiting through the weekend felt like waiting through eternity. In his description of purgatory, Dante neglected to include waiting over the weekend for medical test results. We were completely unprepared for the prospect of a special-needs child—we were blindsided. During the weekend I juggled looking in on Meghan and William and taking care of Paul and Caroline. We survived, but I was not up to the task. The kids were so excited and Meghan was recovering from surgery. William was in full-time neonatal care. He was just less than two pounds and had a challenge eating enough to maintain his body temperature. He also had some jaundice. While it was not touch and go, it was close.

During the weekend we attempted to gather our wits. Each day was a logistical challenge. With the kids at home, Meghan at the hospital, and William in NICU, it was a fragile tripod of love, anxiety, and fear. The prospect of a special-needs child generated a great deal of apprehension and concern. But it was knowing that we didn't yet know that made it such a challenge. The surgery was hard on Meghan, but not as painful as not being able to have William with her. The kids visited her and I visited William. It was a fatigued divide and conquer.

A pleasant surprise was a new friend in the NICU. Her name is Heidi Harper. We were so lost and confused. She was so wonderful and helpful. Her husband Jeff is the older brother of my childhood friend, Elizabeth Harper. Over the weekend we began to learn how premature and fragile William was. We could hold him for only a few minutes at a time, and aside from that, it was classic hospital activity: sit, stare, and wait.

The test results came back as positive. William did have Down syndrome. We had little idea what that meant. But, we knew our plans were changing. Less than a year earlier I had looked at the landscape of my future and saw a happy, fun life for the four of us (Meghan, Watson, Paul, and Caroline). The landscape had changed with the presence of a third child. A third child with special needs was an entirely different view—and it would be different for all of us, Paul and Caroline included. We met with someone from the hospital and were given some reading material. The news was so confusing, and there was so much to consider and an absence of time in which to consider it.

We quickly learned about the vast potential complications that Down syndrome children have. William, it seemed, had many of these challenges. The first we became familiar with was an incomplete intestinal tract. This created a blockage and made eating, and therefore growing, problematic. He had surgery only a few days after birth. His remarkably small size made this a life threatening procedure, even if it was successful. We prayed and worried and prayed and waited. This pattern was repeated often. We did not get better at it, only accustomed to it.

In advance of the surgery, we had a priest come and welcome William into the church with a personal baptism. It was a sweet moment and generated an authentic family experience. In a world where there is little you can do to help, it felt simultaneously hopeful and desperate. There was some satisfaction in being able to *do* something and complete it as planned. There was also some peace gained, as we knew that there were no guarantees with William. There was no future yet that was exciting to look to, nor was there a conclusion that we could imagine.

William survived the surgery—more relief than celebration. Yet, relief is a winner. Meghan was feeling better and recovering; the kids were now used to going to see William at the hospital. I had gotten some sleep. My colleagues Charles and Van had totally taken care of *everything* at work and would continue to do so. The school was remarkable in its support and care. In addition to surviving, William held his weight and then gained a few ounces. This was the news to celebrate. Most days we could hold him for a bit. He had become a slightly heavier two-pound baby boy. Thank God.

We could only be in a crisis for so long before the crisis became our new normal. Meghan came home from the hospital, which was wonderful. The kids became accustomed to our daily trips to the NICU.

The normal day had three trips: before lunch, before dinner, and evening. While we were at the hospital, we had very little to do, and when we were home, we wanted to be at the hospital.

During this time our friends continued to reach out and support us. One day I found a meatloaf on my truck seat (that is *the one* I will remember forever). I never thought meatloaf would bring me to tears, it did.

During our stay in the hospital, my friend and his wife had their baby. Thankfully the birth was uneventful. The view he had of his future had remained constant since that day in his office. Mine had changed dramatically and drastically, several times. Little did I know, the alterations to my personal landscape's horizon would continue unabated.

While we did discover a new normal, it was fraught with uncertainty and fear. There was little to no planning or anticipating anything beyond another day of survival. Following his operation William began to gain some weight. The NICU treated him so wonderfully; they worked and worked to get every bit of food and fat into him. Days were filled with the hope that he would reach three pounds. It was an odd but exciting goal. The days of the week disappeared and were replaced with numbers. There was no Tuesday, only day eight. It was one day at a time.

To say that William was closely monitored would be an understatement. Paul and Caroline called him "wire man." He had wires connected to him each day and every day of his life. These wires soon detected a heart problem. His heart could give out soon if he didn't have an operation—a difficult, risky operation. And of course his size exacerbated the challenge. To qualify for the procedure he would need to weigh five pounds. We had a limited amount of time to bulk him up so he could have the operation. He would die without it and could not have it unless he was bigger. We were literally in a race against time.

Working and watching a two-pound baby grow requires great patience and a strong belief in the process. The growth is imperceptible. The NICU staff was diligent. They acted like they were constantly topping off a gas tank at the filling station with the highest test fuel possible. William got the highest fat and calorically-dense milk on earth. There were moments when it was fun to watch him eat and sleep, knowing we were making progress. Yet, in the back of our minds, we also knew that the clock was ticking.

As we considered which hospital to engage with, we had an instructive conversation with Dr. Henry Miller, a cardiologist from Winston-Salem, who was also my neighbor growing up. We spoke with him about success rates. He paused, exhaled, and told us that the only success rate was *our* success rate. All comparisons from his perspective were not meaningful. Either our experience would be successful (life) or not (death). He encouraged us to get to know the people we would work with. That would have an impact no matter the outcome.

There are not many heart surgeons who work on infants as small as William. We were first directed to Duke. Our second option had a personal connection. A friend from Maine ran the children's ward at a hospital in Charleston, South Carolina. When we reached out to him he was so gracious and encouraging that we wanted to learn more. A personal connection felt right. We felt positive that both hospitals were excellent and appropriate choices. However, we liked the idea of a personal connection. That someone would know us and care for William beyond his status as a patient was a comfort. It would be personal for us, and that reciprocity resonated positively.

I also had a great friend in the area. Because only Meghan and I would be making the trip between Asheville and Charleston, knowing there was support and care in the community was also a comfort. Having someone else to talk with during William's hospital stay sounded good to me. When your infant child is life-threateningly sick, it's a challenge to retain perspective. The days and weeks blur together. Self-care, like nutrition and exercise, gets thrown out the window. A contemplative prayer life turns into a fear-based bargaining request and demand session. A pendulum-like day of ups and downs is overtaken by non-stop worry and more worry. There was very little laughter to soften the edges of day after day of uncertainty and little to do, with much in the balance.

So we waited and fed William. Each day we peered into the future. Each day we estimated when the heart defect would kill him while projecting when his weight would exceed five pounds. We used days to count: He would not live 50 days. The lines crossed at 45 days. We stayed in touch with the hospitals. The surgeon in Charleston was confident, in the way surgeons and fighter pilots have to be.

While William was in the hospital, we had family come to help. It was wonderful to have someone to help with Paul and Caroline. We would have a moment to get some rest or take a walk. Conversations were a mixed bag, as the field of our attention had been plowed and plowed. So much attention to William's plight, yet, so little information to work with. My brother, Fred's, visit stands out, as he could help me to laugh. There was an ESPN commercial with sexual overtones. It was introduced with the line "this goes out to our male audience ages 5 to 95" and it broke me up. It was a welcome release.

We worked hard to remain hopeful. However, there were days when only doom and death appeared in the future. One day I went for a walk with my friend Van Kussrow. I spoke openly with him of my fears that William would die, that his conditions were so dire, and he was too small to endure both the complications and the medical attempts to save him. I wondered aloud if I could get life insurance for him and whether that was prudent or horrid. I never followed up on that thought. But I recall talking about it and that somehow Van listened and supported my wondering without endorsing a path.

William's world was largely unadorned. He lived in a warm plastic bubble: we called it his apartment. They did let us put a toy or two in with him. One was a very old bear of mine. The other was a small dog that my sister, Ruth, gave him. It was a beagle, like our childhood dog Floho; and it was a comfort to see each day.

The fact that it came from her and reminded me of Floho was a potent and surprising source of strength. And given that good feelings were hard to come by, her gift to him consistently generated them—a gift to be grateful for day after day.

And on it went. The days passed. William gained weight. The decision day grew closer. The lines grew closer and closer together, like an introductory lesson in calculus. Except, these lines would touch if we did not act. The day came when we made the decision to go to Charleston. On day 39 of our life together, we would leave Mission Hospital in Asheville, just the three of us, William, Meghan, and me. It was at once liberating and terrifying.

Meghan and William flew to Charleston in a medical helicopter. After weeks of fattening William up, he was quite close to five pounds. We were hopeful about our trip. It was the first time William had left the hospital. I stayed at the hospital and watched them depart.

As soon as they lifted off, I ran to my car to drive to Charleston. I felt like I was in a race. Not that I thought I could outpace a medical helicopter; rather, I was racing to be with them as soon as possible. It is intimidating to be in a new place, much less a hospital preparing for heart surgery on a five- pound infant, so I desperately wanted to be with Meghan. My drive was uneventful. It was lonely. This was before cellphones. Being apart felt like being underwater … I was holding my breath until we were reunited.

It was a whirlwind when I arrived at the hospital. William had been checked in. Our friend had met Meghan and made certain all was well. Friends of my parents had agreed to have us stay at their condominium, so we exited the hospital and made our way there. It was as if we had swum across a great lake and could finally collapse in a heap on the shore, gasping for breath and grateful for solid land.

Greeting us on that shore was the fact that the next day was our eighth wedding anniversary.

MARGARET

In April of 1966 I was four years old. We lived in Ramseur, North Carolina. This was the year my sister Margaret was born. My parent's wedding anniversary is April 4th, and on April 5th of that year, little Margaret died—the day following their anniversary. Like William, she had two older siblings, me and my sister, Ruth. Like William, she was sick and challenged as soon as she was born. I was so young I only remember her echo in my life—the echo of what might have been; the sound from a future that never resonated.

PHONE CALL

We woke up on our first day in Charleston. It was October 26, 1999, our eighth wedding anniversary and the first full day in William's new hospital. Our plan was for an easy morning. It was sunny and still warm in Charleston. We would settle in at the hospital and prepare for heart surgery. Dinner with friends who were in our wedding was nice to think about. My mother had come to town to help us with her friend's condo. All our attention was focused on getting to the hospital and the surgery. We were finally exhaling.

The phone rang while we were still in bed. It was the hospital. Something had happened and we had to come right away.

It was, in fact, an emergency.

Startled and confused, we dressed and departed. We were so new to Charleston that we did not make a fast or efficient trip. This was before the era of the smartphone and the luxury of talking in transit. We knew that William was in trouble. Our minds assumed the worst, or what we thought was the worst.

The worst we could imagine was that his heart was beginning to fail—that we had waited too long for the surgery. As is consistently the case, the worst things are well past our imagination. They are things you would *never* worry or fret about. They are things you do not see coming. These uninvited and unannounced tragedies knock us down and take our breath away.

William was dead.

The hospital had made a medication error and killed him. His medication was in such small amounts that they made a mistake, and the error was more than his tiny system could stand. Our friend who worked at the hospital came out when we arrived and explained everything: All the attempts to save William, the remorse of the poor medic and his own valiant, but vain efforts were shared in complete transparency. We were in shock. Our tiny, sick, 40-day-old son was dead—not from his illness but by a human error.

We had a chance to see and hold William. A lifeless infant is a sad corpse to hold. But, it was our concluding embrace. It was odd at first because he had no wires. All his brief life he had been connected to wires. He was constantly monitored and observed. But now, they brought him to us in a private room, freed from all that circuitry. We held him and cried. We cried and held him. Like all corpses, he seemed empty. The life that had been in him had vanished—gone to wherever lives go. My mother had come to the hospital as well, and she joined us and held him. He was so small, and his time with us had been inexplicably brief.

Just like that … in an instant … gone.

WHAT TO DO . . .

Many times in life we don't know what to do. And at this moment in our lives, we were numb and scared and angry. Nothing made sense. There I was in a hospital room with florescent lights holding my 40-day-old dead son. My wife was there with me. We needed each other so completely, and yet I was so empty and vacant. Eventually, we literally handed over William's corpse. It was the saddest end of an embrace in our lives. All that he was … was gone. If I had felt better, I would have felt dead as well. Bruce Springsteen sang, "Wounded and not even dead." That captures it.

There is a great deal to do following a death. No matter the age, the body must be cared for; and, in our case, a funeral must be arranged. My mother agreed to stay behind and take care of the hospital details. Meghan and I packed our things in a numb, lifeless trance and left Charleston for Asheville. The fury and purpose of my drive down was bookended by the indifference and passivity of our return trip. We had prepared for and worried about so many eventualities—but not this, not even once.

On the return drive we talked about how to tell the kids, our families, and our friends. How could we move forward? A murmur of hope was provided by our two children at home. They would continue to need us, and that would help ground us as we landed. Their life would give some normalcy to William's absence. At five and two they would be sad but would quickly move on to their lives with us. Meghan and I benefitted from our time together in the car. It was the most time we had spent together in weeks, and having each other was a blessing. But this was absolutely *not* the anniversary day we had imagined.

We collapsed upon our return. Meghan's mother had come down from Connecticut to stay with the kids. When we woke up there was much to do. We had to share our news and prepare for a burial. We told family first and then friends. We made arrangements to bury William in a family plot in Ramseur, NC. My Dad's cousin Reverend Mike Jordan would do the graveside service. There would also be a service at the local Catholic Church. These activities kept us busy and were a blessing.

I was so grateful for all who came. It is an opportunity to see the best in people, and not least those who traveled far to grieve with us. Three of my friends traveled: Lewis, Downs, and Arthur. Lewis came from Washington, Arthur came from Winchester, VA, and Downs came from Tampa. It was a comfort to see them, and they just wanted to help. I remember we did some yard work together—how odd. I must have needed the distraction and wanted to make them feel needed. My Dad is a great one for using work or labor as a vehicle for time together. In retrospect, I wish I had hugged them more.

The formal service was in Asheville at St. Eugene's Catholic Church. Our friend Eric Wall played organ for us, which was touching and a wonderful connection for me. It was a long drive from Asheville to the gravesite in Ramseur—close to four hours. William was buried next to my sister Margaret. My parents bought the plot when she died, and they plan to rest there themselves. There was a small graveside service. Many family members came to be with us. William was cremated, and his ashes were put in a small wooden box that came from my Uncle Henry and Aunt Margaret. It was a comfort to include a personal connection in the hereafter.

Life, in part, is like walking toward and into a lake. When you are born you are at the back of the line. In fact, the line is so long, you do not even know what you are in line *for*. Everyone on earth is in front of you. Soon you realize that most of the time we are surrounded by the same people. Our parents are in front of us; our grandparents are in front of them, 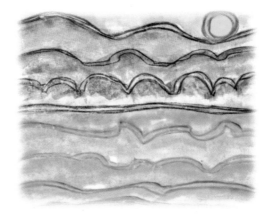 it's a hierarchy of age. As we approach the lake we notice that people walk into the lake and disappear. Not a big worry, as we are far from the lake. Then someone we know goes in, and we wonder, "What happened?" But, there appears to be a sequence. First, a grandparent dies and then younger folk appear behind us. Just like that, we are in the midst of a pack. While the disappearance is not comfortable, you get used to it. People in front of you disappear. People behind you remain. That is just how it is.

Until you bury a child. Then the entire system upends itself. A dear one so close to you and behind you is snatched from the line and hurled far, far into the lake, passing so many who are patiently waiting or living. Everyone is alarmed; they are sad for the infant and suddenly more concerned about their own place in line—fear that the disappearance can be caught like the flu. They want to help, but at a safe distance. The entire system is unnerved. It takes more than a minute for the comfortable illusion of normalcy to return. Things look the same, but it all feels different.

Not only does it feel different, it is different. Underneath our armor there is a giant hole like a shotgun blast, ragged and pockmarked. Sometimes a hole can heal and no scar will remain. Death is not like this, it leaves a mark. There is some healing, the bleeding stops, healing occurs, it transitions from a wound to a scar. But it leaves a mark. Some things leave a mark.

At first this bothered me. I did not want a mark. I wanted to heal and move on. Little did I know that the mark was the best thing I could retain. We need our marks and scars. They remind us of who we are, where we have been, what we have done, and who we have loved. They call to us to keep living and to keep becoming. A reminder that our lives are living testaments to what has come before and what will one day be.

A cloudless crystal blue sky was the stage for our return trip to Asheville following the funeral. To our surprise there was

an immense double rainbow in front of us during the drive. Everyone saw it. This type of rainbow is rare. To a person, we thought it was William, thanking us for his brief life and wishing us well.

Beyond that, I have always thought it was Margaret and William together. The rainbow was comfort, my infant sister and infant son together in Heaven. Perhaps Williams's presence provided a bit of relief for Margaret. Rainbows today pack special meaning— a wink from the hereafter from the two of them.

Williams's headstone is modeled after Margaret's. It is simple. We had the granite cut and carved on Vinalhaven, Maine. Meghan's family has a place there on the Reach; in Maine they call it a camp. I found a part of myself there. The fact that in

Ramseur, North Carolina, there is *literally* a piece of Vinalhaven, makes me smile. Getting that to happen was a feel-good moment in a time where there was not much to feel good about.

When we returned from the funeral, we gathered and braced for the storm to conclude. People returned to their normal lives, guests departed, the days grew shorter, and we were stuck with a weary hopelessness: The bitter, smelly, wretched fatigue that follows an epic loss. We took it with us everywhere, and everywhere we went we were surprised that it was there—a companion we could neither embrace nor evade … purgatory.

DEATH IS HARD ON THE LIVING

Death is hard on the living. That is what I learned. Wherever the dead go, their hardship on earth has concluded. But those of us who love are left in a gigantic, steamy caldron of pain and mystery. Much of the pain comes from the end of an imagined future. When this conclusion is sudden and the person is younger, the pain is different from the future we had imagined as lush and expansive. Similarly, the mystery is more confounding. *Why* is a lingering question that cannot help but be asked and, in the end, has no reason to be answered. William's death left us with many more questions than answers. The questions are either what kills you or what saves you;  it depends on the questions. One day the questions were killing me. It was in late autumn. It was overcast. The days were getting shorter and colder. I was sitting in the living room, looking out the window, drinking coffee, and wondering why, asking all the wrong questions over and over: Like the elementary school mimeograph machine in mind- numbing repetition—bang, bang, bang. Then I was saved. From deep in my soul came the statement, "You can sit and drink coffee looking out the window as long as you want…. But once you get up, you can never come back." The permission to stay made a difference.

I never went back to the window. I wish I could say that I started asking better questions. I did not; that self-inflicted torture continued. But, what I did do was get busy. I got out of the house. I went on walks. I drove places. I listened to the kids more. I did more—I took more action. I tried to think less. One wonderful product of action is it takes energy, which leads to physical fatigue. This produces more and better sleep. I've heard the expression that sleep is God's workshop, so the sleep eventually leads to healing and a gradual return to a productive life. Leaving the window was *the* turning point for me. I was lucky.

I certainly hadn't known then that spending the dark, overcast afternoon with coffee at the window was my nadir, the point which I was not sure I would return from. After that I began to make progress … I began to heal. William died in October, so following his death it was turning to winter. On the car radio one morning I heard a news story about a man who had died in his car overnight. It was bitter cold and snowing. He lost control of his car and went off the side of the road. He never got out of the car.

He was frozen solid when he was discovered. As I listened to the story, I thought about his poor family. One day this man was driving home—the next day he was dead. No goodbyes or farewells. It was a tragedy. Then I understood that each day in the Asheville paper there is a tragedy. Sadly, often more than one. At that moment I felt like I was one of many. I no longer felt isolated in my grief, apart from humanity. Rather, I felt included, a part of the human race. I will never forget it. Today I think of it as the beginning of the end of my grieving.

In retrospect, a key element of this moment was the re-introduction of thinking about others. Grieving is a personal process and inherently self-directed or centered. Being in the world and thinking of others is a powerful way to move forward. There is, or appears to be, a chasm between the immobilized self-centered state and the fluid, healthier state that includes others. The attempt to cross the chasm makes all the difference. The attempt … the trying … the desire … these fueled the change in me. That, after all, is what needed to change—me.

In preparation for William's arrival we had purchased a house and moved off campus. It was a fun and happy remodel. When we finished and moved in, the home had the right number of rooms for our growing family. Four rooms for Meghan and me, Paul, Caroline, and our unborn son. In the wake of William's death, we had one room too many. Meghan's mother stayed with us for a few days. One day when she asked how I was, I just broke down, sobbing that we had one room too many. The process of re-acclimating our home for the four of us, rather than five took a while. There is still a haunted feeling in the house for me. Not William's ghost, but the ghost of the future that was ripped away. A time that never came.

WRECKAGE

Once I came back to life, I looked around at the wreckage left in the wake of William's death. There were sizable medical bills and horrible questions. What do you do when there is nothing to do? We could not bring William back from the grave. He had been killed by his caregivers. Braiding justice, grieving, and healing together is a daunting task. Almost as daunting as not doing the weaving.

We had two major challenges on the practical side of the fence. First, we had significant medical bills from the hospital. Second, we had a potential loss of life lawsuit for the hospital where William died. I did not know what to do, did not even know where to start. Sometimes miracles happen with little to no prayer. One had to do with our hospital bills. Anne Coxe, the school librarian, unbeknownst to us, managed a trust for this type of challenge. One day she pulled me aside and let me know that they could take care of our Asheville hospital bills.

Her kindness to us was not uncommon. A great hardship or tragedy provides a powerful context for bringing out the best in people. We saw this repeated consistently. People rose to the occasion. They reached out to us. They were kind and thoughtful. An element of the librarian's gift and kindness was her humility. She did not make an event out of the gift. Quietly, Anne just pulled me aside and told me about her family's account/trust with the hospital and assured me they would take care of it. We never heard another word about the massive hospital bills or from her family. It was a remarkable act of generosity done with absolute humility.

What remained was the at-fault death in the Charleston hospital. The topic was uncomfortable to discuss and explore. Of course the hospital had an interest in closure as well. We met with an attorney and learned more about the legal perspective. It was awful to work on, and yet it was the only thing we could work on. I knew that doing a great job at this would ultimately not be healing. I also knew that if I didn't do my best, I would regret it forever. Slowly, I learned more. It was horrible learning, the kind of education no one seeks to acquire.

There were three main participants in this process: the hospital, the press, and the lawyers. This was a state hospital and was governed by state regulation. There was a special department that handles situations like ours. The lawyers knew the law and the unique paths toward a beneficial outcome. The press wanted a story and was motivated to share information for the public good. Tough to find a North Star to bind us together and pull us forward.

The hospital had made the error and caused the death. They were forthcoming from the beginning. They helped us find the right person with whom to explore this topic. Sometimes we wondered if there was more to the story than we knew. Perhaps there was. But when we tried to think of what could be worse than what actually happened, it was not easy to imagine anything worse than it was. We never met the person who made the mistake and do not even know the name. It seemed the admirable path to take.

We spoke with one lawyer, and he was very helpful in our understanding of the regulations in such matters. Having a conversation about how much a life is worth, including the variable of Down syndrome, was awkward. But I was determined to understand the context. So I kept asking the next question. Additionally, I have two fraternity brothers who are lawyers, and they were very kind in helping me vet what different people said about the law. They were a great light in a time of darkness.

In addition, our long-time family attorney, Don House, was consistently available through the entire ordeal, both as a counselor and advisor. He was hesitant to provide advice. But at each turn I would ask, wonder aloud, what should I do? Without fail, he was on target with the art of decision making. Because determining when to take action and when to hold back and learn more is certainly an art. At each turn he shared decades of experience with us. He consistently understood the urgency and the irrelevancy of our feelings to the actual situation. At once he provided brilliant counsel and insightful friendship.

The context was a ceiling in the state for cases like ours. The ceiling in this case was a total fixed amount, a *do-not-exceed* figure, a maximum. There were two regulatory variables: The nature of the wrongful death was the first variable. Was the death completely the fault of the hospital? Or were there mitigating contributing factors? In our situation, it was completely the fault/responsibility of the hospital. Loss of earning potential/lifetime wages was the second factor. This variable was much more difficult to gauge for William. We had no idea how long he would have lived or what level of independence he would have experienced. As a special-needs child, his life was on a unique path. These two factors were what drove the financial decision. And it was an odd type of calculus.

The local press was a third entity to consider. The hospital was in favor of maintaining privacy about the death and its details. I imagine this desire was a combination of embarrassment and public relations. Part of the negotiation included discretion in this matter. On the other hand, we took seriously the benefit to society of sharing our story, yet that included the detriment we would experience by becoming public figures. We felt this tension and discussed it. There were three times when a reporter called, and the conversation was so distressing that we declined. In the end we decided to keep our ordeal private.

The process took a long time. Eventually, the state offered us a significant amount. We vetted this, which felt both prudent and greedy. It was a no-win; but, our willingness to do the research left no regrets in our wake. There was a dread in saying yes, as that was one step closer to the land of "Now what do we do?" Our friend Don House was so helpful in this process. He helped us ask hard questions and come out with a more satisfactory outcome. What a gift to have his clear, experienced head on the team. Furthermore, when you receive an award there are better and worse ways to spend it. It's admittedly temping to take it all and indulge. Thankfully, Don helped us diversify the award to our, and the children's benefit.

WHAT NOW?

The conclusion of the negotiations marked a transition. We took a trip, thanks to my parents. Our life began to return to an uncomfortable pattern. We began to get used to a dead son in our wake. We certainly found that life kept going. My return to work, Paul and Caroline's school lives, holidays, all of the earmarks of regular life. In fact, it was the exact life we enjoyed less than a year prior. And yet, nothing was the same. It was the same pair of pants, but they didn't fit anymore.

Most people have a deep need for things to make sense, to understand. Some things are impossible to understand. When this happens, there's a conflict. That is the case in our situation. This intersection, or overlap, is how people lose their minds and go crazy—completely insane. The lack of concert between the way things are and the way we think they should be is Miracle Grow for one of two things: insanity or spiritual growth. Often, and in this case, it was some of both.

There is comfort in knowing that things work out. It is common for this dynamic to play out in a short time span. I gave a talk during chapel at our school about this. The title was "Sometimes There is no Thursday." The idea I presented was that sometimes an event that is confusing on Monday makes sense on Thursday. For example, someone loses their job on Monday; they are shocked and upset. On Tuesday they're at the local convenience store and decide, on a whim, to buy a lottery ticket. Then, of course, on Thursday they win the lottery. Instantly their world makes sense again. They had to lose their job in order to win the lottery. Order has been restored to the universe.

What do we do when there is no Thursday? Not even the shadow or aroma of a Thursday experience? The first thousand or so responses are frustration and angst. As mentioned earlier, this either induces insanity or drives us forward, forward toward a more thoughtful, hope-filled perspective. One day it dawned on me that my understanding was only important for my ego and that to let go meant developing a belief that things can make sense or be good without my understanding. This was a touchstone for a more meaningful faith.

Believing that things are okay without understanding, or despite evidence to the contrary, is a slightly ajar door to a *much* larger and more expansive world. There is an adolescent or juvenile quality when one says I will accept this, when the options are to accept or go insane. However, when the acceptance begins to transition to an embrace, that's where freedom, or relief, resides.

One way to picture this growth or transition is with a pie chart that details the Serenity Prayer. "God grant me the serenity to accept the things I cannot change, the courage to change the things I can, and the wisdom to know the difference." It's my inclintion to begin with

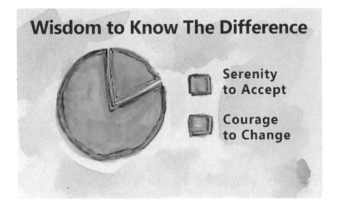

the impression that I need a great deal of courage, because I *can do* so very much. This perspective both overvalues how powerful I am and undervalues how powerful the universe (insert preferred title: Great Spirit, God, Source, etc.) is. From this vantage point, I am responsible for almost everything. That is a tough chair to sit in.

After William died, my pie chart changed (and continues to change) radically. The truckload of powerlessness came with an initially misunderstood

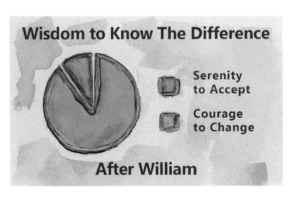

dose of humility. As I grew following his death, I saw more and more that a benevolent element of his life was the stare-down with powerlessness and the embrace of humility. As the part I am responsible for shrunk in size, so did the toughness of the chair. What I can influence or do is modest. This allows me to spend more time on tasks and activities that are, in fact, meaningful. It would not be surprising if the chart continued to change over time, with my part, what I think I can change, continuing to shrink. Likewise, the serenity to accept the influence of the Almighty continues to expand. After our time with William, my ability to believe that this influence, outside of me, is benevolent and uplifting continues to grow. I wish I knew more about how William's death could lead to my increased belief in a benevolent power in our world. Logic would say his death might have decreased my belief in goodness and that I would cling to a vile, hopeless, bitter perspective. Happily, logic does not rule our lives.

One thing I recall is my deeply powerful desire to discover the meaning in his life. I could not believe his life was void of meaning. That was the launch point for this growth … I could not fathom that his life was meaningless. This seed of hope and longing grew and became my mission. William never got to live the life that he might have. My mission became helping others have lives that they would not have had otherwise, without the person that William helped me become. The corner we turn when our self-seeking turns outward toward others is the corner where my belief in benevolence began to grow.

An additional difference between the two pie charts is volume, the amount of impact that can occur. When I believe I am close to "all there is," it generates a limit on the potential output. However, as my part gets smaller, or becomes closer to right-sized, the potential for output soars—often well beyond anything I could have imagined. Seeing this dynamic and believing it more and more empowers my perspective and willingness to try new things, to take risks, to live more fully. When I held William's lifeless body, I did not see this coming—that my world view would be so beneficially refined.

Another change I implemented following our life with William was in the questions I asked or the comments I made. People have hard times and it is natural to reach out to them. It was a blessing that so many people reached out to us. However, the most common question people ask was, "How are you feeling?" Answering this question hundreds of times a day is like ripping a 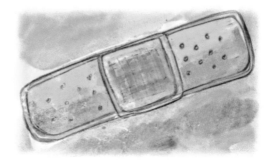 Band-Aid off a wound each time, and at the end of the day, it's more destructive than healing. Today, I just want people who are suffering to know we are thinking about them. So I replaced the question "How are you feeling?" with the statement "We are thinking about you and want to help."

This adjustment is an example of how we were impacted by William's life and death. The death of a child is a powerful event in a marriage. It seems that it can either propel the marriage forward with a shared experience or unravel the union completely. We were fortunate. We were able to work together to locate and appreciate the value in William's brief life with us. I think there were three parts in this: Mine, Ours, and Yours (Meghan's).

YOURS

Witnessing someone else grieve a major loss is heart-wrenching in itself. There is a saying, "A sorrow shared is half a sorrow, a joy shared is twice a joy." In a marriage that has lost a child, the shared sadness does not always divide itself. For example, when one spouse shares the grief with the other, the impact over time can be injurious rather than healing. Immediately after William's death we depended on each other completely. As the days passed, it became clear that each of us needed to grieve independently … *and* we needed to grieve as a couple.

This was hard. Specifically, it meant that much of my grieving needed to be done without or away from my wife, Meghan. Our grief had become too co-mingled to heal. This is the nature of a mess; it needs to be simplified before it can be sorted. The mix of emotions and responsibilities make healing from a death challenging in the best of circumstances. Marriage is at once a humbling and uplifting relationship. Yet, in the end, I (we) sorely lack insight to other people's lives. To this day, I could not say what Meghan's experience was like. Sure, big descriptions like sadness and pain are shared, but in a way those are short on actual meaning. And the significant work of putting ourselves together again is really an inside job.

On my best days I would make certain Meghan knew I loved her and let that stand, independent and concise. On bad days I could ignore her completely, or worse, spend all day trying to cure or save her. The challenge of understanding a person is infinitely more difficult when a couple is grieving together. It is hard to help and easy to damage.

One distinct challenge is when one person starts to feel good again. For example, if I was feeling better, there would be a moment when I would see Meghan and feel guilty about feeling better. Thoughts like, "Why are you feeling good, your son died … you should feel bad" would plague me. Or, if I was enjoying the day and Meghan came to me to share her sadness, I might have an irritated response such as, "Why are you bringing me down, I was just starting to feel better?" At one point it became clear that the path forward included a bigger team of friends and family to shoulder the load of our grief and support our return to health.

As you might imagine, this is easier to describe than implement. Each spouse occupies the specific vantage points on a rotating basis. It became clear that we needed to expand our support system beyond ourselves, and in most cases, beyond our immediate families, with whom the same dynamic exists on a less pronounced level. This means close friends are essential. Close describes the emotional connection as well as physical proximity.

Being able to have coffee with a friend is a winner both for the connection and also for the change of venue; it is beneficial to leave the house.

We stumbled and bumbled through this as I suspect most couples do. I certainly wanted to have it both ways. I wanted Meghan to talk with her other friends, as I was tired of hearing it. Yet, I wanted her to listen to me. This is the precise tension of grieving as a couple: you depend on each other, yet it's critical that we relearn how to expand our dependency. We found that for our marriage to survive, we had to work at this expansion of dependency. It was a tightrope between stifling interdependency and painful neglect and abandonment.

It would be nice to offer a magic way to move forward as a grieving couple. We never found it. It did help when I realized that we did need to grieve both as a couple and as individuals. That knowledge gave us a chance to work on it. Death and grief are sloppy. No getting around it. Grieving is sloppier as a couple … but not as lonely.

SCHOLARSHIP

As we returned to regular life, laughter returned. We thought more about the future. We invested more energy and passion in what Paul and Caroline were doing. Work returned to a daily activity with pleasures and responsibilities. There was a comfort in life's ebb and flow. As we settled into our new life, though, it felt odd. Little more than a year before I had looked at our life with satisfaction that we, the four of us, would enjoy what lay ahead. Now, after adjusting the picture to life with three children, then life with a third child with special needs, then to life with two living children and one dead, and finally to life with two children and one in Heaven, it entailed a great deal of transition that concluded at the same place we began. It was the same view of the future, but we were radically altered by William's short life.

The problem (or opportunity) is that you have a broken heart, just shattered. No matter the circumstance, the dreams of a future have been smashed on the rocks of physical events. Gravity has pulled lives into a labyrinth of consequences and outcomes. Part of grieving and a return to living is digging out and then turning what you have into what you want. It starts as a mess and, if we are fortunate, it winds up being a cathedral for our pain and our dreams. Like any structure, it takes a plan to get started, and then you must cultivate momentum. Whatever elegance there is can only be found in retrospect.

There was a moment after we returned to what we might call "regularly scheduled programming" that I knew there was more to do with and for William. My thoughts continued to return to education. One day, while running at the track, it came to me. William never got to have the life he might have had. Someone who got a better education would get to have a life they would otherwise never have had. I needed to build a scholarship at my school. A student who gets a better education … wow, it makes a massive difference and is a life-altering experience.

A scholarship fund is a noble ambition. Like all funds it requires money. Our dear friend Betsey Ambler helped us found a scholarship at the Asheville School. The founding is easy to do, the funding is another matter. So I decided to create a fundraising triathlon. I liked training for events and I liked the story of making William's life meaningful by helping others have a life that he never had. We would get sponsors for the triathlon to fund the scholarship. The idea was straightforward. Contact a hundred people and ask them to help. The fundraising was simple enough. We are fortunate to have many friends and colleagues. They all wanted to help us when we suffered, but there was nothing to do. The response was humbling.

Next, we needed a course. Arthur Kearns lives in Winchester, VA, and he volunteered to put together a course: 1K swim, 10K bike, and a 5K run. While I was training, our son Paul decided he wanted to do it with me. What a gift. I had to get into the pool and re-teach myself how to swim. I had swum before, and was very comfortable running and biking. I had never done all three together. The training was also a nice conversation piece when I would call for financial support. I enjoy training. That made the entire process much more fun. My best friend Frank made T-shirts for us.

When we drove to Winchester, it was a fun trip for me and Paul. I liked that he was getting to know Arthur, who's one of my closest friends. We went to high school together and then shared a house in Washington, DC following college. He had been training as well and commented that he enjoyed swimming again. It was a beautiful day, and the swim was easy, as was the bike ride. There was no crowd of onlookers, just the three of us, and it was more like a fun community experience than a race. The run was a bit of a challenge. As the day progressed it became hotter, and we became depleted. We had to stop and refuel in the shade and cool down with a wet washcloth. But, we finished up right: Paul sprinted to beat me at the tape. That night we ate a feast. The fatigue was wonderful and the relief palpable. Training and working for months had produced a wonderful sense of meaning and an admirable outcome. We raised over $10,000 and founded William's scholarship. It was greatly meaningful for me to create something that helps others, a profound step forward in living a rich, full life.

Sometimes public acknowledgement can create a strong sense of existence and pride. The school's advancement office noticed what we were doing, and Travis Price wrote an article in the school magazine. I was touched. So often we work and work and never know if anyone cares or even notices. This article certainly created in me a welcoming sense of belonging and being appreciated. I felt a little less wounded as a result of it.

We sponsored the triathlon as a fundraiser twice more. Both times the event was held on the Asheville School campus. Each time we raised more money, Frank gave more T-shirts, and more people participated. It was so fun and so humbling. People wanted to help and were happy to have an event to train for. Paul ran it every year, and as he got older, he got much faster. In fact, he became a track star in high school and ran competitively at Bates College. The only reason we stopped sponsoring the triathlon was that my position at the school was eliminated. When we left the school, we had raised more than $80,000 for William's scholarship fund. Every year a child receives tuition assistance and attends the Asheville School who would not have attended without our help. It is satisfying that a student gets to have a life that they would not have without William.

KENYA

As we built our new life outside of the school environment, the energy I had spent working on the triathlon needed a new place to live. I traveled with my children during this time. We took both children to each continent. This was a tremendous investment in them and in our relationship and was a wonderful experience. Traveling with our children was one of the best decisions of my life.

The idea came to me when we were in Maine on vacation. It came to me out of the blue and clear as a bell. It was as close as I have come to an inspired vision: The picture was taking both Paul and Caroline to each continent. They were each around 14 when we began. Our travels together made wonderful memories and added strong and lasting insights into their perspective on the world. Additionally, these trips wove remarkable threads into the fabric that is our relationships.

Caroline and I had a magical safari in Kenya. The children I saw in Africa made an impression on me, that they needed help. There were many places where water and food are not readily available. But, perhaps more importantly, there was a shortage of schools, and where there were schools, they were short on teachers and supplies. Later, when I was traveling for work, I had the great pleasure to attend several WE Charity days. WE Charity is a non-profit organization that helps children provide aid and support around the world. I attended three in total: Toronto, Minneapolis, and Vancouver. At each one I was at a behind-the-scenes event prior to the festivities. They have a program in which you can fund a school as part of their five-pillar program in community building. When I first heard about it I thought how remarkable it would be to build a school. At the second one, I had the thought of building a school for William. At the third WE Charity day, I stepped forward and made the commitment. I was going to fund a schoolhouse in Kenya in William's memory.

Fundraising for the schoolhouse was similar to my efforts for the triathlons. Asheville School had been willing to allow us to build a scholarship fund, though the project was neither embraced nor shunned by the institution; it had a sweet awkwardness. WE Charity, on the other hand, was an engaged partner that was prepared with fundraising, web-based tools, and support for our outreach. Working with them was a wonderful experience.

So we began. I sent e-mails to everyone I knew. I posted to Facebook and asked friends to promote as well. We called people, and soon the money began to pour in. It was fantastic that WE Charity provided a landing page and took credit cards. It made it much easier for people to give and for us to track. Our initial goal was $10,000, which would fund a schoolhouse, part of their five-pillars program. The other pillars are medicine, water, agriculture, and commerce/economy. They believe that these five areas create a sustainable foundation for a village to grow and prosper.

Our friend Dale Neal heard about our efforts working to create meaning from William's life and death. He was a reporter for the local Asheville paper. He came over with a photographer, took pictures, and interviewed our entire family. He wrote a wonderful article.* There is something galvanizing about being in the paper. It made our work seem somehow more real. It was a powerful, legitimizing force, just like the article Travis Price had written for the school magazine.

* http://www.citizen-times.com/story/life/2015/10/30/short-life-inspires-african-school/74597772/

We soon surpassed our original goal of $10,000. We decided to keep going and follow our plan for the project. In retrospect, this is a reminder that there are times when the project or cause becomes substantial and takes on a life of its own. This was the case with the Kenya school. I had waited years and been unable to start, and then BANG! When I gathered myself and hit the go button, away we went. In the end, we raised $18,226 for the schoolhouse.

And then the miracle happened.

WE Charity came to us and said they had a matching grant for our project. This brought the total benefit for the project up to $36,452. They asked us how we wanted to apply the funding. We decided to focus on a single village and fund all five pillars. By funding the additional pillars, we had the opportunity to name or honor someone for each pillar. This was fun.

We named the Health pillar after Frank Hintz's father. Frank is my best friend, and he was with me every step of the way: He supplied the T-shirts for the triathlons and was critical in my regaining momentum in the weeks following William's death. We named the Food and Agriculture pillar after Will Graham and Rock Amick's fathers. Both are friends from college who have always been there for me in thought, word, and deed, when I have struggled and when things have gone well. The Water pillar we named after my infant sister Margaret. As I have written, she died the day after she was born, and the day after my parents' wedding anniversary—just like William. My hope was that this would be meaningful for my parents. The Economic pillar we named after my friend Amos Kearns.* He was a contemporary of my father's, and we became friends as I struggled to make it on my own in my 30s.

*http://www.sprinklecaldwell.com/news/rich-in-strength/

So, in the end, we financed an entire village in Kenya. The name of the village is Irkaat.* As of this writing, I have not visited, but I look forward to spending time there and reading to and with the children. I never dreamed of things going this well. The entire project went much better than planned. All that was required was that I kept doing my part. As small as it was … that made all the difference.

* http://www.sprinklecaldwell.com/irkaat-kenya-school/

TODAY

Today our life has found a new normal. We have embraced "William," the Egyptian hippo figurine from the Metropolitan Museum of Art, as a mascot. Our son, Paul, has the hippo tattooed on his leg

with William's name and birthday. We have Christmas ornaments and key chains with our mascot. These are reminders of his time on earth and his place in our life.

Surviving the death of a child as a couple deserves and requires a great deal of grieving and healing. There are three elements that must heal: spouse A, the couple, and spouse B. Mine, Ours, and Yours. I have written what the process looked like from my perspective. It is important that I remember how limited our insight into another person's grief and healing actually is. As part of a couple I am responsible for what I am able to bring to the table. As I grieved and then began healing, I needed to bring both the new health and the remaining pain to the table of our marriage. I needed to be cognizant of time, neither skimping on nor indulging in my grief.

Additionally, his death impacted both of our children. Meghan and I were different parents following William's time with us. I hope we have been able to fold what we learned into our life as a family. Without a doubt, how we think and feel about the world and each other was also refined and nurtured.

In the end we stopped long enough to heal, but not so long that the wound would fester. We acted enough to keep our momentum, but rested enough to survive the ordeal.

INFORMATION ABOUT GIVING

Want to do something to help?

The first and best suggestion is to look in your own community, find something that resonates with you, and get your hands dirty. If you prefer to help us, here are options:

I.

William Peter Jordan Memorial Fund

North Carolina Community Foundation
3737 Glenwood Ave.
Suite 460
Raleigh, NC 27612
919-828-4387
800-532-1349
https://www.nccommunityfoundation.org/

Online giving:
https://donatenow.networkforgood.org/nccf
(identify William Peter Jordan Memorial Fund)

II.

Asheville School

Those wishing to contribute to the Fund can write a check to

Asheville School

Attn: Advancement Office
360 Asheville School Rd.
Asheville NC, 28806
(put William Peter Jordan Scholarship in the memo, or enclose a note)

Online giving:

www.ashevilleschool.org

(identify William Peter Jordan Scholarship in the comments)

III.

WE Charity

"WE Charity empowers change by providing communities with resources that create sustainable impact. We do this through domestic programs like WE Schools and internationally through WE Villages. The unique partnership with ME to WE, a social enterprise, ensures that WE Charity achieves a remarkable rate of financial efficiency. This means that on average 90 percent of donations go directly to life-changing programs that inspire youth and provide transformative outcomes that help break the cycle of poverty."

To continue William's legacy and learn more about how you can help shift the world from "me" to "we," visit online at www.we.org/donate.

Made in the USA
Columbia, SC
22 January 2020